# Holidays and Holidaymakers

## DEBORAH ELLIOTT

Wayland

Titles in the Into Europe series include:

**Energy**
**Environment**
**Europe's History**
**Farming**
**Holidays and Holidaymakers**
**Industry**
**Life in Europe**
**Transport**

**Picture Acknowledgements**
Chapel Studios 17, 29; Ecoscene 19; Eye Ubiquitous 4, 6 (both), 15, 26, 34, 43,
44 (bottom); Tony Stone Worldwide *cover* top (Robert Frerck), bottom (Bruno De
Hogues), 9, 10, 13, 14, 18, 20, 24, 27, 28, 30, 31, 32, 36; Topham Picture Library
7, 16, 22, 40, 41; Zefa 8, 11, 12, 21, 23, 37, 39, 42.
All artwork is by Malcolm Walker.

Designed by Malcolm Walker
Cover pictures: top, A view of the sea front of Benidorm in Spain.
bottom, The Arc de Triomphe in Paris lit up against the night sky.

Text based on *Tourism in Europe* in the Europe series published in 1992.

First published in 1994 by Wayland (Publishers) Limited
61 Western Road, Hove, East Sussex BN3 1JD

© Copyright 1994 Wayland (Publishers) Limited

**British Library Cataloguing in Publication Data**
Elliott, Deborah
   Holidays and Holidaymakers. - (Into Europe Series)
   I. Title  II. Series
   306.4

ISBN 0 7502 1047 8

Typeset by Kudos
Printed and bound by G.Canale & C.S.p.A. in Turin, Italy

**Errata**
Page 6: The caption at the top of the page should read, 'Having fun splashing around in the water! These holidaymakers have chosen to visit the sunny Costa Brava in north-eastern Spain.'

Page 11: The second sentence of the second paragraph should read, 'Marbella is a resort on the Costa del Sol in the south, Benidorm is a resort on the Costa Blanca in the east.'

# Contents

# Where shall we go?

Many people spend their holidays in Spain. There, they can visit beautiful and historic towns like Madrid, Seville and Granada. Or they can relax on one of the many sandy beaches and swim in the warm sea.

▼ *Holidaymakers enjoy Spanish festivals, called fiestas. The Spanish people dress in traditional costume and there is music and dancing.*

▲ *The countries of Europe have different landscapes and climates.
Holidaymakers have a lot of choice about how and where to spend
their holidays.*

*Having fun splashing around in the water! These holidaymakers have chosen to visit the sunny Costa Brava in southern Spain.* ▶

Which is your favourite type of holiday? Do you like soaking up the sun on a hot beach? Or do you prefer skiing or walking in the mountains? Perhaps you like sports such as windsurfing, sailing, climbing, cycling or horse riding? Maybe you would rather visit a city with historic buildings and interesting places to visit?

You can find almost any type of holiday you can think of in one or more of the countries of Europe.

◀ *Crete is an island off the south coast of Greece. Holidaymakers who visit the island can enjoy the warm weather and beautiful beaches. They can also experience traditional customs, such as spinning wool by hand.*

▲ *This photograph of holidaymakers in an English seaside town was taken over seventy years ago.*

*You may think it was a cold day because people are wearing hats and coats. But few people wore bathing suits in public in those days. It was considered very daring!*

*The number of hotels in certain European countries and the number of times the hotels were used for one-night stays in 1991.* ▶

| country | number of hotels | number of overnight stays |
|---|---|---|
| Belgium | 2175 | 7736 |
| Denmark | 941 | 9017 |
| Germany | 18642 | 134699 |
| Greece | 4410 | 44235 |
| Luxembourg | 234 | 997 |
| Netherlands | 1923 | 11595 |
| Portugal | 320 | 20272 |
| Spain | 3728 | 138719 |
| TOTAL | 32373 | 367270 |

◄ *Skiing holidays cost a lot less now than in the past. So, more and more European holidaymakers can enjoy the fresh clean air and beautiful scenery as they ski down the mountain slopes.*

▼ *This chart shows the percentage of people who spent holidays in particular European countries in 1991.*

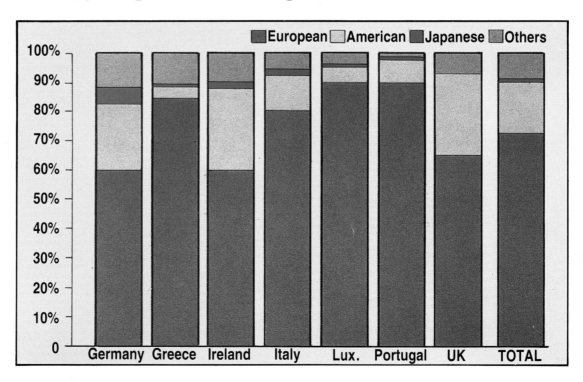

▲ *Seeing the sights of Bruges by boat! Holidaymakers who visit the pretty Belgian city can sail along the many canals and admire the historic buildings.*

# Sun, sea and sand

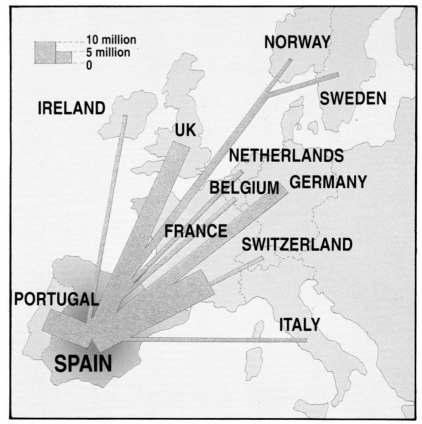

Holidaymakers looking for sun, sea and sand in Europe can choose from the hundreds of resorts in the Mediterranean. The Mediterranean is the name given to those countries with coastlines on the Mediterranean Sea - such as Spain, France, Italy, Greece and Turkey.

The photograph opposite is of Marbella and the one below is of Benidorm. Both are holiday resorts on the southern coast of Spain. You can see how popular both resorts are by the number of people packed on to the beaches. Look at how many high-rise hotels and apartment blocks have been built specially for holidaymakers in Benidorm.

Spain is one of the only countries in the world which has more visitors each year than people living there. The chart opposite shows where most of the visitors come from.

Spain has been popular with holidaymakers since the 1950s. In fact, tourism is now the country's main industry. Once small quiet towns and villages have become huge noisy holiday resorts.

The Maltese Islands lie in the Mediterranean Sea, between Sicily and the coast of Africa. There are five islands - Malta (the largest), Gozo, Comino, Comminotto and Fifla.

Over the past thirty years Malta has become very popular with holidaymakers. There is only one large hotel on the island of Gozo, so not too many people can visit at one time.

Before holidaymakers started to visit Malta and Gozo, the main industry on the islands was fishing. The fishing harbour in the photograph is in Gozo. It is typical of many villages there and in Comino. Now tourism is the main industry. Many Maltese people work in hotels and restaurants, or make lace, pottery and crochet goods to sell to the holidaymakers.

Lots of hotels, nightclubs and restaurants have been built specially for holidaymakers.

▼ *Athens is the capital city of Greece. Thousands of years ago, the ancient Greeks built theatres, and temples for their gods on top of a steep hill called the Acropolis, in Athens. The remains of some of the buildings are still there today. Millions of people visit them each year.*

Greece lies in the south-eastern corner of Europe. The coastline is long and rocky with thousands of inlets and bays. There are also many Greek islands. Some of them are now run almost entirely for tourism.

▼ *Holidaymakers in Greece love to eat traditional dishes in the tavernas (restaurants) which line the harbours and beach fronts. Traditional Greek dishes include tsatsiki, a mixture of cucumber, yoghurt and lemon juice, and dolmades, which are vine leaves stuffed with meat or vegetables.*

▲ *Some holidaymakers like the places they visit so much that they buy holiday homes there.*

*This couple bought a windmill in the Greek island of Crete. They have turned the windmill into a holiday home and spend a few weeks there each year.*

Tourism is one of the biggest industries in Greece. Lots of hotels, nightclubs, restaurants and shops have been built for the 8 million holidaymakers who visit Greece each year.

France is one of the largest countries in Europe. There are many different places to visit and sights to see for the millions of people who visit the country each year. There are many beautiful rivers and forests, too.

Holidaymakers can stop off in the city of Paris, where they can see the famous Eiffel Tower and Notre Dame Cathedral.

In winter, skiers can ski down the many slopes in the snow-covered Alp Mountains.

◄ *This modern block of holiday flats is in La Grande Motte, a resort on the south coast of France.*

▲ *Many British holidaymakers visit the Canary Islands, especially Tenerife, Lanzarote and Gran Canaria.*

*The islands are small and have a particular style of architecture. People are trying to make sure that any new hotels or apartment blocks are built in the same style, and do not look out of place or spoil the environment.*

Because the Mediterranean is such a popular holiday area, there are plenty of jobs. However, the environment in the area is under threat from holidaymakers who leave litter on the beaches. Also, sewage from holiday resorts is pumped into the Mediterranean Sea, causing pollution. In fact, it is unsafe to swim in some parts because the water is so dirty.

◄ *Would you like to sit on this beach or swim in the water? Thoughtless people have left rubbish on the beach. The broken glass and rusty tins are dangerous for swimmers and fish.*

▼ *The photograph below shows an area of Marbella beach. Sewage has washed up on the shore. If something is not done to stop the pollution, Marbella could become a holiday resort which no one wants to visit.*

# Up in the mountains

▲ *These holidaymakers are watching a game of winter polo in the Alps. Polo is like hockey, except players are on horses.*

The Alp mountain range stretches over 1000 kilometres across south and central Europe, from France through northern Italy, Switzerland and Austria to north-west Slovenia.

Skiing is the most popular winter sport in the mountains of Europe. Holidaymakers can enjoy the fresh mountain air as they race down the snowy slopes.

Switzerland and Austria have many ski resorts in the mountains. The resorts are mostly towns and villages which are hundreds of years old. Holidaymakers from all over the world come to see the beautiful scenery and take in the traditional atmosphere.

◀ *After a tiring day on the slopes, skiers can visit one of the many bars or cafés in the resorts and enjoy a hot drink.*

▼ *Les Arcs is a ski resort in the French Alps built specially for holidaymakers. The mountains around Les Arcs offer a wide choice of slopes to skiers, and there are lots of bars, nightclubs and restaurants in the resort. However, some people prefer the hotels in traditional Swiss and Austrian villages to the modern hotel and apartment blocks in Les Arcs.*

Austria is a country in central Europe with lots of mountains and forests. It is well-known for its ski resorts, like Kitzbühel (below), Söll and Schladming.

The towns are hundreds of years old and have lots of very old buildings and churches and pretty cobbled streets. Many years ago, skiing was one of the only forms of transport for people living there.

Up until a few years ago, a ski holiday in Austria cost much more than most people could afford. Today, prices are lower and thousands of holidaymakers take winter holidays in Austria.

The ski towns and villages have changed as hotels, shops, restaurants and ski lifts are built for the growing number of visitors. Towns like Kitzbühel, which were once small and quiet, are now major holiday resorts.

The high mountain ranges of the Mittelland, the Alps and Jura Mountains cover almost one-quarter of Switzerland. Holidaymakers can enjoy the views of tall snowy peaks, beautiful clear lakes, rushing waterfalls, thick forests and icy glaciers all year round. They can ski, skate or toboggan in winter, and walk and climb in spring and summer.

In winter, rivers and lakes are covered in thick ice, which is perfect for skaters. In summer, when the ice melts, the lakes offer all sorts of water sports like water-skiing and sailing.

◀ *This is a view of the Bernese Oberland mountain range in Switzerland. Holidaymakers come here to enjoy the beautiful scenery and for the clean fresh air.*

Iceland is an island in the North Atlantic Ocean. It is visited by many Europeans every year. It has many icy glaciers and areas of snow all year round. Visitors can also see the many volcanoes and hot springs.

▼ *This photograph is of a hot spring in Iceland. The inside of the Earth is very hot. When the heat rises, it turns to steam which collects in pools of water, called hot springs. Hot springs usually happen in countries like Iceland, which have lots of volcanoes.*

▲ *Any visitor to Iceland must visit this wonderful waterfall. You can see just how big it is by looking at how small the people beside it look.*

*This waterfall is not just for holidaymakers, though. It is used to make energy. The force of the water is used to drive machines in power stations, which make electricity.*

▲ *There are many different landscapes in Iceland. This pretty forest is at the foot of a tall, craggy mountain range.*

▼ *Sporting holidays are also called activity holidays. This man is trying to beat the rapids in Iceland on a canoeing holiday.*

Mountain holidays are becoming as popular as holidays in the sun. However, the growing number of holidaymakers in Europe's mountains is harming the environment.

Trees and forests are cut down to make way for yet more ski slopes and holiday resorts. Modern hotel and apartment blocks are built in old traditional villages, causing the price of property to go up and spoiling the look of the environment.

# City sights

▼ *Night-time in the Tivoli Gardens in Copenhagen, the capital city of Denmark. Over 250,000 people come to the Tivoli Gardens every year. There, they can walk around the beautiful gardens and enjoy the huge fairground.*

*The River Seine flows through the city of Paris in France. Boat trips run along the river taking visitors past some of the famous sights of this romantic city.*

*Here, a boat passes the historic Notre Dame Cathedral. Imagine how many people must have visited Notre Dame during its 800-year history.* ▶

Paris is one of the most famous cities in the world, and one of the favourites among holidaymakers. It is thought to be a very romantic city. The French call their capital 'The City of Lights' -  a city with lots of things going on, day or night.

Paris has lots of well-known museums, art galleries, statues and buildings. In fact there are simply too many to list. The Eiffel Tower, the Champs-Elysées, the Palace of Versailles and the Louvre Museum are only a few.

Since the beginning of the 1990s, political events in the countries of Eastern Europe have brought about many changes. Before, the governments of many of the countries did not welcome influences or cultures from other places. People in the countries had little opportunity to travel.

Holidaymakers have always enjoyed the beautiful, interesting cities of Eastern Europe. Prague in the Czech Republic, Budapest in Hungary and Moscow in Russia are just three shining examples of cities rich in history and culture, with lots of places to visit and things to see and do.

Moscow is the capital city of Russia. It dates back as far as the eleventh century. Its most well-known building is the Kremlin, which holds the offices of the government, three cathedrals, and the palace where the Russian royal family lived many years ago.

◀ *This building looks as though it could have come from a children's fairy-tale. In fact, it is part of St Basil's Cathedral in the centre of Moscow. The unusual domes are called 'onion' domes.*

A holiday in one of Europe's spa towns holds much interest for many holidaymakers. They visit places like Bath in England (opposite) and Igalo in Montenegro (below) to bathe or drink the local spring water. So, what is so special about the water?

Since Roman times, people have believed that spa water from the local springs has important minerals which help cure certain illnesses and are good for our health. The water is thought to be especially good for people with back problems, or who suffer from arthritis. Holidaymakers have flocked to the spa towns, hoping that all their aches and pains will be washed away.

The towns began to grow as hotels and restaurants were built for the growing number of visitors.

▲ *At the height of summer, many of Rome's millions of visitors pause for a well-earned rest at the city's famous Spanish Steps in the Piazza di Spagna.*

Hundreds of years ago, when the Roman Empire controlled much of Europe, Rome was the most important city. It is still very important, as holidaymakers come from all over the world to visit the many famous historic buildings, museums and fountains.

▼ *The photograph below could be of a smart restaurant, or a dining room in a top class hotel, perhaps. In fact, it is a café in a railway station in Hungary.*

*Now that Hungary has opened its borders to visitors from other countries, more holidaymakers can enjoy the history and architecture of this Eastern European country.*

▲ *Visitors to the town of Madurodam in the Netherlands are in for a surprise. It is a model town. All the buildings are tiny copies of those in a real town. There is a library, a school, shops and parks.*

The Italian city of Venice is built on 117 islands and mud flats in a lagoon. The city does not have ordinary roads. It has canals which link the islands. Barges carry goods, and motorboats and gondolas carry passengers along the canals. Gondolas are long graceful boats.

*Holidaymakers gather in St Mark's Square in Venice.* ▶

# What's next?

▲ *The Pyrenees is a range of mountains between France and Spain. The mountains are high, rugged and very beautiful. They are home to many birds and animals, including the rare chamois, or mountain goat, and a species of eagle only found in the Pyrenees.*

*Huge areas of the Pyrenees have been turned into National Parks. A limited number of visitors are allowed into the parks, in order to protect the environment.*

The photograph below is a scene from a performance by the Russian Bolshoi ballet company. The Bolshoi dancers travel all over the world, appearing before millions of people.

The Russian government gives a lot of money to the Bolshoi and other ballet companies in the country, to help pay the costs of training, costumes and travel. In this way the government is encouraging visitors to come to Russia to experience this cultural delight.

*◄ This vulture is very rare. Thanks to the money made from visitors to the French National Parks, the vulture and other wildlife can be protected.*

Holidaymakers bring lots of money to the places they visit, and, as a result, help to create jobs for the people of those places. Holidaymakers help in other ways too. Better roads and more shops, restaurants and facilities are built for them, which can be used by local people, too.

Travel gives people the chance to learn about other cultures, eat different foods and experience other ways of life.

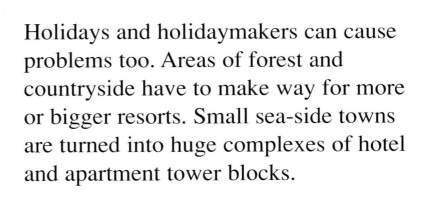

Holidays and holidaymakers can cause problems too. Areas of forest and countryside have to make way for more or bigger resorts. Small sea-side towns are turned into huge complexes of hotel and apartment tower blocks.

◀ *Many holidaymakers like to see some of the traditional customs of the places they visit. However, some people feel it is wrong to dress up in local costume and perform just for the amusement of holidaymakers.*

*In country areas of Europe, such as in southern France and Italy, farmers can sell their fruit and vegetables to holidaymakers staying in local camp sites or villas.* ▶

▼ *Holidaymakers pause for a rest during their visit to Ephesus, the remains of an ancient city in Turkey.*

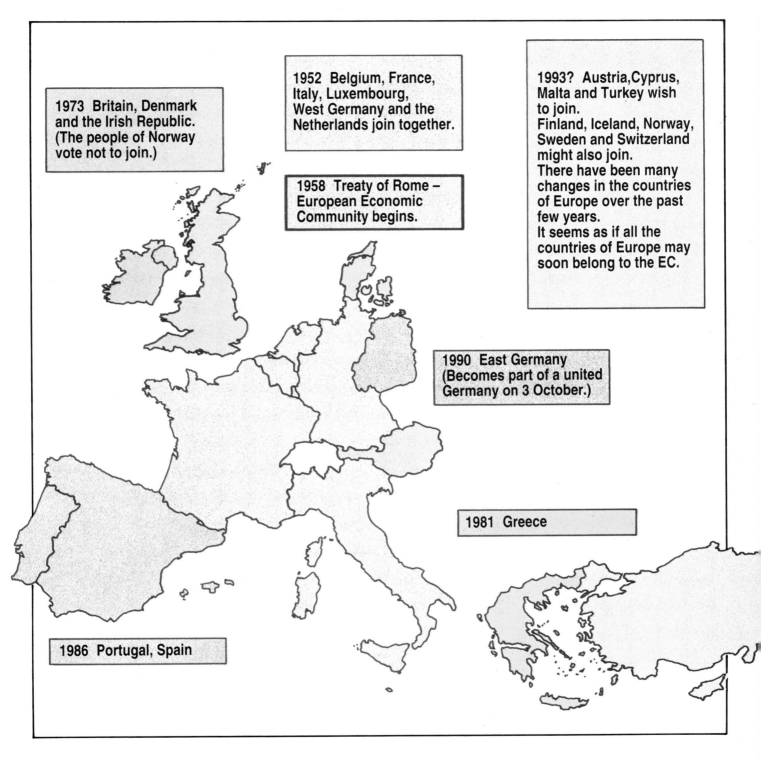

**1973** Britain, Denmark and the Irish Republic. (The people of Norway vote not to join.)

**1952** Belgium, France, Italy, Luxembourg, West Germany and the Netherlands join together.

**1993?** Austria, Cyprus, Malta and Turkey wish to join.
Finland, Iceland, Norway, Sweden and Switzerland might also join.
There have been many changes in the countries of Europe over the past few years.
It seems as if all the countries of Europe may soon belong to the EC.

**1958** Treaty of Rome – European Economic Community begins.

**1990** East Germany (Becomes part of a united Germany on 3 October.)

**1981** Greece

**1986** Portugal, Spain

▲ *The countries which belong to the European Community.*

# Glossary

**architecture**   The way buildings are planned and how they look.

**customs**   Ways of doing certain things which have been around for many years. For example, festivals and ways of dressing.

**environment**   The world around us. For example, animals, plants, rivers, mountains and the air we breathe.

**European Community (EC)** A group of countries in Europe which have joined together to come up with ideas and plans for farming, industry and tourism.

**facilities**   Places, in a town, city or holiday resort where people can go and have fun. For example, swimming pools, libraries, theatres, cinemas and restaurants.

**glaciers**   Huge rivers of ice.

**historic**   Very old and full of history.

**landscape**   The way an area or country looks. For example, if there are mountains, rivers, forests or deserts.

**percentage**   The number out of every 100. For example, 10 per cent means 10 out of every 100.

**pollution**   Things that spoil the environment.

**rare**   An animal or plant is rare when there are not many of its type left in the world.

**resorts**   Towns where people go on holiday.

**traditional**   Things which have been done for a very long time.

**volcanoes**   Mountains which can explode and throw out hot ashes and burning rocks.

# More information

## Books to read

*A Taste of France* by Roz Denny (Wayland, 1994)
*A Taste of Italy* by Jenny Ridgwell (Wayland, 1993)
*Inside France* by Ian James (Franklin Watts, 1988)
*Inside the Netherlands* by Ian James (Franklin Watts, 1990)
*Italy* by Daphne Butler (Simon and Schuster, 1991)
*Our Country* series (Wayland, 1991-2)

## Useful addresses

If you would like more information about holidays in Europe, you could write to these organizations.

Commission of the European Communities
8 Storey's Gate
London SW1P 3AT

Council of Europe
Boîte Postale 431 R6
67006 Strasbourg Cedex
France

# Index